A Note from
Mary Pope Osborne About the

MAGIC
TREE HOUSE®
FACT TRACKERS

When I write Magic Tree House® adventures,
I love including facts about the times and
places Jack and Annie visit. But when readers
finish these adventures, I want them to learn
even more. So that's why we write a series of
nonfiction books that are companions to the
fiction titles in the Magic Tree House® series. We
call these books Fact Trackers because we love
to track the facts! Whether we're researching
dinosaurs, pyramids, Pilgrims, sea monsters, or
cobras, we're always amazed at how wondrous
and surprising the real world is. We want you
to experience the same wonder we do—so get
out your pencils and notebooks and hit the trail
with us. You can be a Magic Tree House® Fact
Tracker, too!

Mary Pope Osborne

Here's what kids, parents, and teachers have to say about the Magic Tree House® Fact Trackers:

"They are so good. I can't wait for the next one. All I can say for now is prepare to be amazed!" —Alexander N.

"I have read every Magic Tree House book there is. The [Fact Trackers] are a thrilling way to get more information about the special events in the story." —John R.

"These are fascinating nonfiction books that enhance the magical time-traveling adventures of Jack and Annie. I love these books, especially *American Revolution*. I was learning so much, and I didn't even know it!" —Tori Beth S.

"[They] are an excellent 'behind-the-scenes' look at what the [Magic Tree House fiction] has started in your imagination! You can't buy one without the other; they are such a complement to one another." —Erika N., mom

"Magic Tree House [Fact Trackers] took my children on a journey from Frog Creek, Pennsylvania, to so many significant historical events! The detailed manuals are a remarkable addition to the classic fiction Magic Tree House books we adore!" —Jenny S., mom

"[They] are very useful tools in my classroom, as they allow for students to be part of the planning process. Together, we find facts in the [Fact Trackers] to extend the learning introduced in the fictional companions. Researching and planning classroom activities, such as our class Olympics based on facts found in *Ancient Greece and the Olympics*, help create a genuine love for learning!" —Paula H., teacher

MAGIC TREE HOUSE® FACT TRACKER

Wild West

A NONFICTION COMPANION TO MAGIC TREE HOUSE #10:
Ghost Town at Sundown

BY MARY POPE OSBORNE
AND NATALIE POPE BOYCE

ILLUSTRATED BY ISIDRE MONÉS

A STEPPING STONE BOOK™

Random House 🏠 New York

For Randy Courts and Jenny Laird,
with love

Historical Consultants:

PAUL ANDREW HUTTON, Distinguished Professor of History, University of New Mexico

JACOB TURCOTTE, English teacher, and the students of Frazer High School on the Fort Peck Assiniboine Reservation

Education Consultant:

HEIDI JOHNSON, language acquisition and science education specialist, Bisbee, Arizona

Special thanks to the folks at Random House: Mallory Loehr, Jenna Lettice, Isidre Monés, Paula Sadler, and Maya Motayne, and gratitude forever to Diane Landolf, our really smart editor.

WILD WEST

Contents

Dear Readers,

In <u>Ghost Town at Sundown</u>, we traveled back over 150 years to the Wild West. The tree house landed in an old ghost town from the 1800s called Rattlesnake Flats. There, we came across wild mustangs, a cowboy named Slim, and even some horse thieves!

After our adventure, we had a lot of questions. Were there really ghost towns, and do they exist today? And what about cowboys, horse thieves, and mustangs? When we began to research, we found out that you can still visit a ghost town, and cowboys and mustangs played a big part

in the Wild West. And there was more. We
read about pioneers who traveled west
in covered wagons and famous outlaws
and the lawmen who tried to stop them.
We learned about Native Americans and
what happened to them when thousands
of people moved into their lands.

This research was another big
adventure! So get out your notebooks
and let's gallop back to a time when
people risked everything to start new
lives. It will be quite a ride!

Jack

Annie

1

Wild West

The Wild West was an amazing time in American history. It began when people settled the American West about 150 years ago. Cowboys, Native Americans, soldiers, outlaws, lawmen, and pioneers who went west in covered wagons all played a part in this exciting story.

The Wild West got its name because sometimes it really was wild. When people first began moving there, it was a wilderness with few sheriffs, judges, or courts, and not even many laws. The Wild West lasted from 1865 to 1895, but the history of the American West began long before that.

In the 1600s and 1700s, thousands of people left Europe to settle in America. Almost all of them lived on the East Coast, along the Atlantic Ocean. When the United States became a country, all thirteen of its states were in the East.

As more and more people came to America, the East got crowded. The U.S. government began thinking about all the empty land in the West. But that land wasn't really empty. For thousands of years, Native Americans had lived there.

The lands west of the states were called *territories* of the United States.

A *territory* (TARE-uh-tor-ee) is an area that the government controls.

When people started moving west, they had a big problem. The trip meant crossing the rugged Appalachian Mountains. The Appalachians stretch from eastern Canada almost 2,000 miles down to the southern United States.

Once there were 60,000 settlers in a territory, it could become a state.

Appalachian Mountains

Daniel Boone

In 1775, the hunter and explorer Daniel Boone led pioneers through a gap in the mountains that became known as the

Cumberland Gap. The opening was large enough for horses and wagons to pass through. Then they could travel farther west.

Daniel and his men marked out a 200-mile trail that had been used by Native Americans. It was called the Wilderness Road and went from Virginia to Kentucky. In the 1770s, thousands traveled the road through the Appalachian Mountains into Kentucky and lands farther west.

Daniel Boone was called a long hunter because he was often away in the wilderness for months.

Mountain Men

By about 1810, trappers and fur traders called mountain men started going as far west as the Rocky and Sierra Nevada Mountains. They worked for fur companies trapping beavers and other animals.

Hat made from beaver fur

Beaver fur hats were very popular.

Almost 500,000 people traveled on the Oregon Trail.

Most mountain men traveled on a trail known as the Oregon Trail. It covered 2,000 miles from Missouri to Oregon. Many pioneers later took this trail, and some went all the way to the West Coast.

Like most Native Americans at the time, mountain men often wore clothes

18

and moccasins made from deerskin. They carried survival gear such as large knives, tomahawks, powder horns, pistols, and rifles. For shelter, the men lived in rough cabins, canvas tents, or tipis. Tipis are cone-shaped tents covered in animal hides. Native Americans on the Great Plains used them.

The men often camped out, even in winter. For food, they hunted deer, buffalo, elk, and bear. Sometimes they ate

Mountain man

berries or wild plants, but mostly they ate lots and lots of meat.

Native people sometimes invited the men to stay in their villages. But many native people wanted these strangers off their lands. They weren't afraid to attack if they thought their way of life was in danger.

Jedediah Strong Smith

Mountain men were tough and brave. One of the toughest was Jedediah Strong Smith. Once, a grizzly bear attacked Jedediah,

Jedediah Strong Smith

breaking his ribs and almost tearing his scalp and ear off. Jedediah talked a friend into sewing his ear and scalp back on. After that, he wore his hair long to hide the scars.

Gold!

In 1848, a worker was building a sawmill called Sutter's Mill on a river in California. Suddenly, something shiny in the stream caught his eye. It was flakes of gold!

News spread that the California hills were full of gold. In 1849, thousands of men headed to California to get rich. Most of them arrived in ships that sailed around South America. They came from the eastern United States and as far away as China!

Trips could take five to six months.

Some made their way over rough, rocky trails like the Oregon Trail. The California gold rush ended in the 1850s, but miners kept coming. There was a lot more gold—and silver—in Nevada and Colorado!

Towns grew up around the mining camps. Some of them became big cities that still exist. Others became empty shells after the mines closed. These are called ghost towns.

Sacramento, California, began as a mining town. Today it's a large and busy city.

America Gets Bigger

As more people moved west, more territories became states. By the 1850s, Texas, California, and Oregon had become some of the first western states. But the West covered half the United States, and there was still a lot of land for farms and towns.

The U.S. government wanted to make the country larger by settling these lands. To get people there, President Abraham Lincoln signed the Homestead Act in 1862. It gave 160 acres of western land to people who paid ten dollars and agreed to farm it for five years.

Families by the thousands loaded up their wagons and headed west. Among the new arrivals were outlaws, lawmen, gamblers, ranchers, shopkeepers, and farmers. The Wild West had begun!

The Red Ghost

The deserts in the Southwest are dry, sandy, and hot. In the 1850s, the army shipped camels from other countries to carry supplies in the Southwest. The idea was that camels would be better than horses in such a harsh climate. They survive for days without water, people can ride them, and they are able to carry heavy loads. Some of the camels got loose and ran wild in the desert.

In 1883, people in Arizona told tales of the Red Ghost. This large hairy beast was supposed to have trampled and killed someone. Farmers who saw it thought a dead person was strapped on its back. People were terrified! Then one day a farmer saw the Red Ghost eating a tomato in his garden. He shot it, and the strange beast toppled over. It was a camel.

2

Native Americans and the Land

Native Americans have lived in North and South America for tens of thousands of years. They were here long before Christopher Columbus came. Because Columbus thought he had arrived in India, he called them Indians. In fact, Native Americans are the first true Americans.

In the 1800s, there were about 200 tribes in the West. The tribes were not all alike.

Each spoke its own language and had its own way of life.

Living Off the Land

Even though the tribes lived in different ways, they had things in common. They all hunted animals for food. Those in the Northwest made their homes near forests, lakes, and the ocean. They lived in

Makah
Nez Perce
Sioux
Tillamook
Ute
Paiute
Navajo
Zuni
Pueblo
Arapaho
Cheyenn
Comanche
Hopi
Apache

The Makah tribe took canoes out in the ocean to hunt whales!

villages, fished, and hunted deer and other game.

Illinois

Wampanoag
Iroquois
Narragansett

Shawnee

Cherokee

Chickasaw

Seminole

It is believed that the Hopi were the first people to live in North America.

Southwestern tribes like the Hopi and Zuni built small villages called pueblos (PWAY-blowz). They grew squash, beans, and corn. They also raised sheep after the Spanish brought them to New Mexico.

Pueblos were usually made of adobe bricks—a mixture of clay and straw.

Navajo still raise sheep today.

Another southwestern tribe, the Navajo (NAH-vuh-ho), came from Canada about 500 years ago. At first, they were mainly hunters, but later they also raised sheep and vegetables. Instead of villages, the Navajo lived in small family groups.

A number of tribes, like the Cheyenne (SHY-an), Comanche (kuh-MAN-chee), and Sioux (SOO), lived on the

Great Plains. The Great Plains are flat, grassy lands covering parts of ten western states all the way up to Canada.

The eastern Great Plains have tall grasses and regular rainfall. The western plains have shorter grasses and not as much rain.

There were about 75,000 people from Plains tribes in the 1850s.

In the 1500s, the Spanish brought horses to America. Some escaped and formed herds of wild horses called mustangs. Native Americans captured some of them and became expert riders. Horses made it much easier to hunt the millions of buffalo that once roamed the plains. The Plains tribes moved from place to place following the buffalo herds.

They used almost every part of a buffalo to make things like drums, belts, and rope. They ate buffalo meat and made tipis and clothes from buffalo hides. They also carved knives and spoons from buffalo bones and burned buffalo dung for their fires.

Buffalo skin tipi

Connection to the Land

Native Americans felt a deep bond with nature. Even though their beliefs weren't exactly alike, most tribes believed that a Great Spirit made the earth. They thought that everything in nature—animals, plants, rocks, and water—has its own special spirit.

Native American ceremonies often called on nature to guide the people. The Hopi and other southwestern tribes danced for rain. The Sioux did a buffalo dance to celebrate the return of the buffalo. They wore buffalo skins to show respect for the animals they depended on.

The buffalo dance remains a part of Sioux culture.

Owning the Land

Most people in the United States believed in the right to own land. They felt people could buy and sell it. Native Americans didn't share this belief. Even though the tribes had special hunting grounds, for them, the land belonged to everyone.

Indian Removal Act

In the early 1800s, the government wanted the United States to grow larger. Settlers began to move to the Southeast. Over 125,000 Native Americans already lived in Georgia, Alabama, North Carolina, Tennessee, and Florida.

In 1830, President Andrew Jackson signed a law called the Indian Removal Act. The law forced thousands of Native

The Trail of Tears was the awful journey Native Americans took to Oklahoma.

Americans, including the Creek, Cherokee, and Choctaw tribes, to move to Oklahoma, which was up to a thousand miles from their homelands.

Manifest Destiny
By 1840, most Americans believed in the idea of *Manifest Destiny* (MAN-uh-fest

DES-tuh-nee). Manifest Destiny meant that the United States had a duty and right to stretch all the way from the Atlantic to the Pacific Ocean. It also meant that, no matter what, this was to be the future of the country.

The government felt that Manifest Destiny made it all right to take land from Native Americans. Congress made agreements called *treaties* with the tribes. The treaties were supposed to protect their lands. But so many settlers moved west that the treaties were often broken. Native Americans were being pushed out of their homelands.

Sitting Bull

Crazy Horse

Sitting Bull and Crazy Horse were the chiefs who led the Sioux in the Battle of the Little Bighorn.

General Custer

The tribes fought back. Sometimes they attacked the settlers or had fierce fights with U.S. soldiers. In 1876, the Lakota Sioux and the Northern Cheyenne fought their last big battle. Former Civil War general George Custer led soldiers into battle on the Little Bighorn River in Montana. Custer was killed, and so were 263 of his men.

Even though Native Americans won this battle, they couldn't hold on to their lands. With the help of the army, the government opened even more land for settlers. Native Americans were forced into areas called *reservations*. They were not allowed to live anywhere else but on the reservations.

End of the Buffalo

In 1869, workers finished laying rails for a railroad that went across the country.

When the railroad was finished in 1869, workers celebrated.

Now even more people could travel west.

Thousands of men worked on the 2,000-mile railroad. When the workers or settlers needed meat or fur, they shot buffalo. People also shot buffalo for sport. Native Americans of the plains depended on buffalo meat for food. Once, there had been millions of buffalo. By the 1890s, only a thousand remained.

The Native Americans of the Great Plains lost the buffalo and a way of life they'd had for thousands of years. Many of them died from sickness and hunger.

The idea of Manifest Destiny worked for the United States. The West had opened up, and millions owned land there. But treatment of Native Americans during this time was one of the most shameful chapters in American history.

3

Wagons West!

In 1843, more people than ever moved to the West. What would you think if you were a kid then and your parents made this decision? Since there were no cars, you'd travel in a wagon pulled by oxen or mules. The fastest the animals could go was only about fifteen miles a day. The trip might take five or six months!

From 1841 to 1869, more than 400,000

people moved to the West. They were known as *pioneers* (pie-uh-NEERZ). Pioneers are the first people to settle down in an area and make it their home.

Wagon train

The families traveled in groups. Each family had its own wagon. When the wagons all lined up, they formed a chain called a wagon train. Some wagon trains were over five miles long!

Many pioneers took the Oregon Trail. This rough, rocky trail went through the state of Missouri and what would later become the states of Kansas, Nebraska, Wyoming, Idaho, and Oregon. It ended in the Willamette Valley in Oregon. From there, people often branched off or kept going to California.

Settling the Great Plains

When people first began moving west in the early 1800s, they settled in Kentucky, Tennessee, Ohio, Indiana, and Illinois. Later, most of the pioneers passed through the Great Plains on their way to Oregon and California.

By 1860, there were about 175,000 settlers in California.

But in the 1850s, many pioneers realized that the plains were good for farming and ranching. They started settling on the *prairies* there. The wind blew nonstop across the grasses in the summer. Winters were usually cold and snowy. Swarms of terrifying locusts (similar to grasshoppers) devoured crops. But the biggest problem many settlers had was loneliness. Houses were so spread out that families had no close neighbors.

Getting Ready

The wooden wagons were about twelve feet long and six feet wide. Hoops held up the white canvas tops, which were oiled to make them waterproof. Edges of the canvas could be pulled together and fastened at either end to keep out

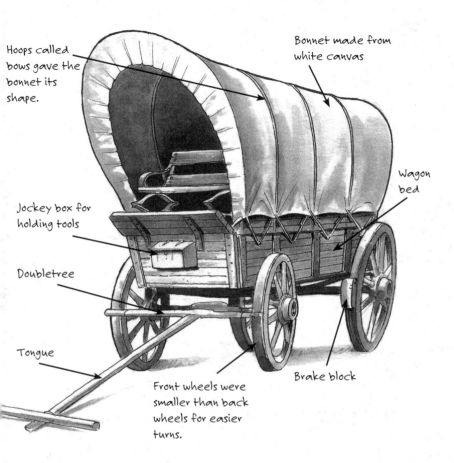

Hoops called bows gave the bonnet its shape.

Bonnet made from white canvas

Jockey box for holding tools

Doubletree

Tongue

Wagon bed

Brake block

Front wheels were smaller than back wheels for easier turns.

rain, snow, sand, and wind. The wagons had strong wheels that could go over bumps.

A fully loaded wagon weighed about 2,500 pounds. That's as much as a team of oxen or mules could pull.

A Very Hard Trip

Pioneers had to take their wagons across raging rivers like the Snake River, in Idaho. They climbed the steep Rocky Mountains and Sierra Nevada Mountains. Sometimes the wagons were too heavy for the oxen or mules to pull. To lighten the load, people threw out their trunks, clothes, pots, pans, and other supplies on the trail.

So many wagons rolled over the trail that it became rutted. The wheels cut such deep tracks that you can still see their marks today.

Wagon ruts

Germs in water caused cholera and typhoid fever.

Even though people took medicine with them, many got sick and died from diseases like *cholera* (KAH-luh-ruh) and *typhoid* (TY-foid) fever.

People might fall under the heavy wagon wheels or drown in river crossings. Although it didn't happen often, Native Americans sometimes attacked the wagons.

Day by Day

People hired wagon masters to guide them. Many were mountain men who knew the trail well.

The day began very early, when the wagon master woke the sleepy pioneers with whistles, gunshots, or a bugle. People took down their tents and loaded their wagons. Women and girls started making breakfast.

People often had bacon, coffee, and biscuits or corn bread.

After the meal, the train moved out. Almost everyone except babies with their mothers and sick or old people walked beside the wagons ... many for 2,000 miles or more!

At noon, the pioneers stopped for lunch and a rest. In the evening, the wagons formed a circle for safety. Campfires glowed, and the smell of food filled the air.

Did you ever hear the expression "circle the wagons"? It means protecting each other.

After dinner, grown-ups chatted and kids played before bedtime. Then everyone settled down in wagons or tents or on the ground for a good night's sleep.

Rivers and Mountains

Getting the wagons across rivers was usually hard. If the water was shallow,

A wagon train crosses the Platte River in Nebraska.

oxen and mules pulled the wagons through it. If it was deep, the wagons might go across on ferries. The animals swam across.

Sometimes people sealed the wagons with tar to keep the water out and fastened airtight barrels to the sides. The barrels helped float the wagons across the river. If the crossing went well, there were often celebrations and everyone danced!

Steep mountains were another problem. The pioneers unhooked the oxen or mules and walked them to the top of the mountain. Thirty or more animals were yoked together on long chains attached to a wagon. The animals pulled the wagon over wooden rollers until they got it to the top. They did this again and again until all the wagons reached the top.

When the trail finally ended in Oregon, the pioneers must have been relieved and

happy. Today what they did seems impossible, but what a great adventure it was!

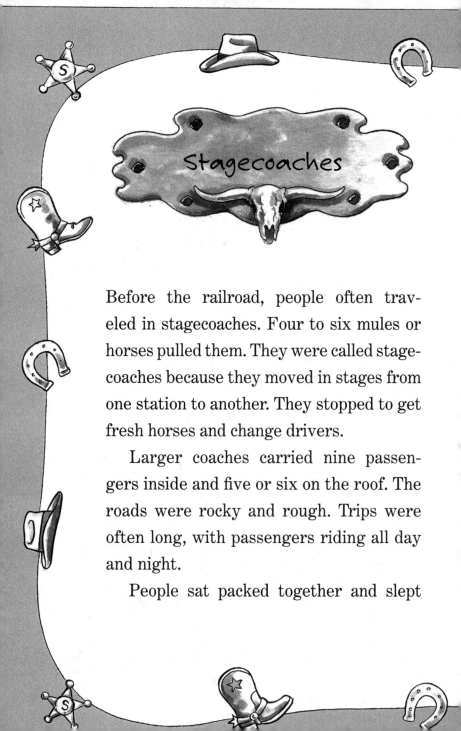

Stagecoaches

Before the railroad, people often traveled in stagecoaches. Four to six mules or horses pulled them. They were called stagecoaches because they moved in stages from one station to another. They stopped to get fresh horses and change drivers.

Larger coaches carried nine passengers inside and five or six on the roof. The roads were rocky and rough. Trips were often long, with passengers riding all day and night.

People sat packed together and slept

sitting up. There was a rule that no one could snore or rest his or her head on anyone's shoulder. There was also a rule that if the horses ran away, passengers should *not* leap out of the stagecoach! But singing was allowed. Yay!

4

Pioneer Life

One of the first things pioneers had to do was to clear their land and plant crops. They also needed shelter. At first, they slept in their wagons and tents. The Homestead Act said that the settlers had to build a small house that was at least ten feet wide and twelve feet long. It was supposed to have at least one window with glass in it.

Pioneers who lived in places with lots of

It was possible to build a log cabin like this in only a few days.

trees, like Montana and Oregon, built log cabins.

The cabins usually had dirt floors and stone fireplaces. People didn't need nails to build their cabins. They cut logs carefully and notched them at the corners to lock them together. To seal the spaces between the logs, they stuffed them with scraps of wood and made cement from mud or sand.

Prairie Houses

Pioneers on the prairie faced strong winds, hot summers, and cold winters. Because there were few trees on the prairie to use for wood, settlers often built sod houses. Sod is grass-covered dirt held together by roots. People cut blocks of sod and used them like bricks.

Large families of eight or ten people might live in one small cabin.

A family stands in front of their sod house in Nebraska.

There were problems with sod houses. When it rained, the roof often leaked, and the dirt floor turned into mud. If the roof got too dry, dirt clods fell from the ceiling. And most annoying of all were the bugs, snakes, and mice that lived in the dirt and sometimes came into the house to check it out!

Work! Work! Work!

Pioneers did almost everything themselves. They planted and sold crops and raised their own vegetables. The men hunted wild game and fished.

Since there were very few doctors, people had to treat their own injuries or illnesses. Women gathered wild herbs like pennyroyal for fevers and used ginger or cayenne pepper for colds. They cured a cough by rubbing the person's chest with skunk oil! Whew!

Wild West Kids

Kids worked long hours every day. Girls as young as five or six sewed, washed, cooked, and took care of their brothers and sisters. There were cows to milk and cream to churn into butter. And when they finished those

These boys are helping their father by pushing a plow.

chores, it was time to feed the chickens and bring in some eggs!

Boys spent long days in the fields with their fathers, clearing the land and planting crops. Since many of the homes were heated with wood, boys had to know how to use an ax, a saw, and other tools. Their fathers also taught them how to repair wagons and mend fences.

Girls often married when they were just teenagers.

Almost every young boy learned to ride and hunt. By the time boys were teenagers, many knew how to run a farm.

Schools

Kids of all ages studied together in one-room schoolhouses. There were no laws in the Old West about how long kids had to go to school. Most of them only went when their parents didn't need them to work at home.

A teacher and her students pose outside their schoolhouse in Nebraska.

If kids needed a drink of water, they took a bucket and filled it from a well or stream.

Schools often went only through eighth grade. There were very few books. Kids memorized their lessons and recited them back to the teacher.

There were both male and female teachers. Some of the teachers were almost the same age as their older students! Beginning around 1845, 600 women went west to teach. The women could not be married and had to live with a family near the school.

Going to Town

Western towns were often very busy. The streets were full of cowboys, farmers, and shopkeepers. Almost every town had at least one bank, stable, blacksmith shop, boardinghouse, and saloon.

Goldfield was a bustling mining town in Nevada.

There were dirt streets wide enough that wagons, horses, and stagecoaches could turn around. Some were as wide as football fields! Sidewalks were up off the ground to keep people from getting muddy when it rained.

Many men went to saloons to play

Gamblers play a card game called farro at the Orient Saloon in Bisbee, Arizona.

cards and drink. As people made their way down the sidewalks, music from the dance halls filled the air. Sometimes gunshots rang out when men used guns to settle their arguments.

Farmers and their families took wagons into town to buy things they needed. Kids ran around playing. Men went to boot shops for new boots or to get their old ones repaired. They met up in barbershops and exchanged news while getting a haircut. Women crowded into stores to buy things such as needles, thread, cloth, and coffee.

Life wasn't all work. People took time out to have some fun. There were parties, church picnics, and county fairs. Women set up tables and opened picnic baskets. Often, there was a fiddler who fiddled away while people danced.

Every year, families went to the nearest town for a Fourth of July celebration. A parade usually wound its way through the streets, and at night, fireworks lit up the sky. People gave speeches, ate picnic lunches, and read the Declaration of Independence. It was a day off from work to celebrate!

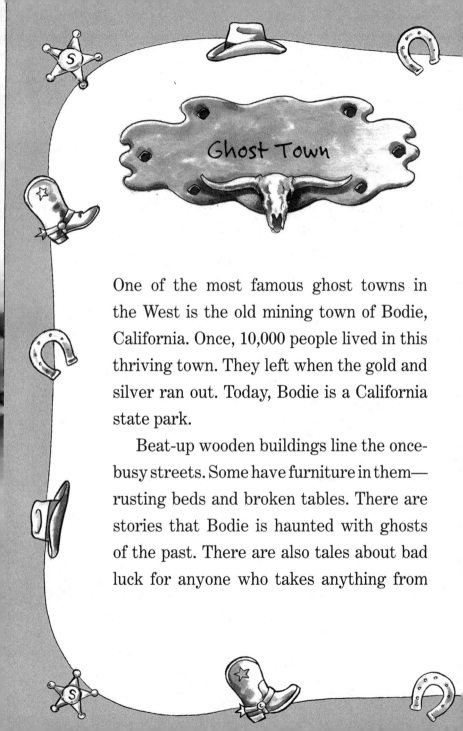

Ghost Town

One of the most famous ghost towns in the West is the old mining town of Bodie, California. Once, 10,000 people lived in this thriving town. They left when the gold and silver ran out. Today, Bodie is a California state park.

Beat-up wooden buildings line the once-busy streets. Some have furniture in them—rusting beds and broken tables. There are stories that Bodie is haunted with ghosts of the past. There are also tales about bad luck for anyone who takes anything from the town, even if it's only a rock!

Imagine walking down Bodie's quiet, windy streets and hearing ghostly voices singing part of an old miner's song: *"Get me some gold . . . get me some gold."*

Bodie, California

5

Cowboys, Horses, and Cattle

Cowboys and the Wild West belong together. When people bought western land, it was often for cattle ranching. Texas, Arizona, Colorado, and New Mexico had some of the largest ranches in the West.

The first cowboys in the United States were Mexican cowboys, called *vaqueros* (vah-KARE-oze), who worked on ranches in California and Texas.

<u>Vaquero</u> comes from the Spanish word for cow.

Ranchers needed help herding their cattle, so they hired cowboys to work on their land. Not all cowboys looked like what you see in the movies. Some were Mexican and African American. They came from all different places.

The men had to ride well enough to throw a rope over the neck, feet, or horns of running cows from the back of a galloping horse. Cowboys were also expected to be expert horse tamers and good at fixing things around the ranch.

The cowboys' lives were hard. They worked for very little pay. In the winter, many rode from ranch to ranch looking for odd jobs until spring came.

Cowboys often spent fifteen-hour days in the saddle. They checked to make sure that the cattle didn't wander too far away and brought strays back to the herd. They also cared for sick and injured animals.

 It takes a lot of practice to rope a cow.

Until the 1880s, there were no fences on the range. Cattle were free to graze wherever they wanted. To keep track of the ones that belonged to them, ranchers burned a special mark on them with a

hot brand. Sometimes cattle thieves put
another brand on top of the old one and
claimed the cow as their own!

The Roundup

Every spring and fall, the cowboys
rounded up large herds of cattle so that
the rancher could sell them and ship

Cowboys usually rode four or five different horses each day.

them on trains. The men spread out on the range to search for cows belonging to their ranch. This often took long days of hard work.

Once they rounded up all the cattle, the drive could begin. When there were large herds, two cowboys rode in front of the herd, four rode on each side, and several followed behind.

A cook wagon had plenty of beans, bacon, and hot coffee!

If the cattle drive began in Texas, it usually ended at the railroad in Abilene, Kansas. The men drove the cows on the Chisholm Trail, which stretched 600 miles from San Antonio, Texas, to Kansas. A cattle drive could take as long as two or three months. Once they reached a *cow town* like Abilene, the cowboys loaded the cattle on trains that would take them to markets in the East.

Towns where the cattle drives ended were known as cow towns.

I just heard a cowboy say he needed grub and was going to ask Cookie for some bear signs!

Oh, Jack, cowboys call food grub. Cookie is the cook. But hurry! I need some bear signs right now! (That's cowboy talk for doughnuts.)

Danger

Being a cowboy was just plain dangerous.
Some were injured or killed when they
fell off their horses and were dragged.
They faced lightning, sandstorms, and
ice storms with no place to take shelter.
And as if this wasn't enough, the men had
to beware of rattlesnakes and swarms of
biting insects.

A new cowboy
was called a
tenderfoot or
a greenhorn.

River crossings could be very tricky.
If the cattle started swimming in a circle,
some of them could drown—and the cowboys, too.

Stampedes were one of the biggest
dangers. When cattle got scared, they
might take off together in a wild run.
During a cattle drive, most stampedes
happened at night. The smallest noise or
movement could start one. A sneeze, a

horse shaking itself, or a rumble of thunder might scare the jittery cattle.

To keep the cows calm, cowboys sang, whistled, or played the harmonica. If the cattle did stampede, the men galloped beside them and tried to turn them in a circle. The smaller the cowboys made the circle, the slower the cattle went.

Cowboys and Their Horses

Cowboy horses often came from mustang herds. A good cowboy horse was strong,

It was risky being a cowboy!

smart, and fast. It could cover about twenty miles without getting tired.

Ranchers usually owned the horses the cowboys used, but cowboys owned their saddles. A saddle could cost a whole month's pay. It might be the most expensive thing a cowboy ever owned. There was a saying that when a cowboy sold his

Cowboys wore rugged clothes that could stand up to the harsh outdoor lives they led.

Bandannas for protection against dust

Hat for sun protection and signaling

Vests with pockets

Leather chaps to protect pants and legs from cacti and scrapes

Guns for thieves and wild animals

Spurs

Boots with pointed toes that could slip out of stirrups

saddle, his cowboy days were done.

Changes

By the 1890s, most ranchers had fenced in their land with barbed wire. The fences kept cattle from wandering away and clearly marked a rancher's land.

As the number of ranches and farms grew, there were fewer places where the herds were allowed to go. Trains began coming all the way into Texas and other ranching states, and ranchers didn't have to travel so far to ship their cattle east. By 1895, the days of roundups and long cattle drives were over.

Cowboy's saddle

Barbed wire is thick wire with sharp, spiky knots every few inches.

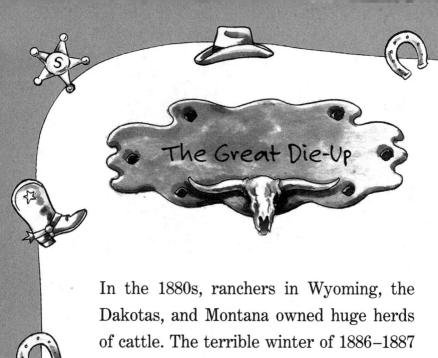

The Great Die-Up

In the 1880s, ranchers in Wyoming, the Dakotas, and Montana owned huge herds of cattle. The terrible winter of 1886–1887 changed this forever.

It had been a very hot and dry summer. Grass dried up, and some even burned, so the cattle were already hungry. Then winter came.

Temperatures fell to fifty degrees below zero Fahrenheit. One blizzard after another swept in, and the cattle couldn't find enough food. Millions of cows starved or froze to death. Ranchers called this winter the Great Die-Up, and from then on, they kept smaller herds.

Drifting Before the Storm
by Frederic Remington

6

Lawmen and Outlaws

A big reason the Old West is called wild is because of its famous outlaws. They broke the law; lawmen tried to stop them. Towns voted for the men they wanted to be sheriffs. Sheriffs chose deputies to work with them. At times, when a sheriff needed to hunt down outlaws, he formed a group of armed men called a posse (POSS-ee).

Because western towns were usually

far apart, it was hard to find enough sheriffs. They could arrest outlaws only in their towns or counties. Outlaws often escaped to the countryside. It was not hard to rob stagecoaches, trains, and banks and get away.

U.S. Marshals

Some of the most famous lawmen weren't sheriffs. They were U.S. marshals. Unlike

 U.S. Marshal Bill Tilghman was a legend for arresting more outlaws than anyone else.

local sheriffs, marshals worked for the U.S. government. They were allowed to go all over the country to catch outlaws.

Judges traveled around territories and states to hold trials.

Guns were not allowed in Dodge City, Kansas.

Even though most people in the West owned guns, in many towns people could not walk around with them. When men rode into town, they had to leave their guns at the sheriff's office. They picked them up when they left town.

A sheriff in Colorado once made rules for his lawmen. One of these rules was that they should not hit prisoners over

Lawmen sometimes put up Wanted posters around town so that people would recognize an outlaw and turn him in.

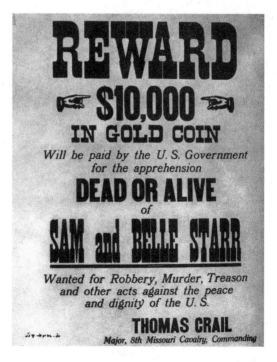

REWARD

$10,000

IN GOLD COIN

*Will be paid by the U.S. Government
for the apprehension*

DEAD OR ALIVE

of

SAM and BELLE STARR

*Wanted for Robbery, Murder, Treason
and other acts against the peace
and dignity of the U. S.*

THOMAS CRAIL

Major, 8th Missouri Cavalry, Commanding

the head with guns because they might break them. (He meant the guns, not the heads!)

Rustlers

Cattle or horse thieves are called rustlers (RUSS-lerz). In one famous case, rustlers stole cattle from ranches in Montana. Then they drove them over the border to sell in Canada. Then they turned around and rustled cattle from Canada to sell in the United States!

There are still cattle rustlers today. In 2015, ranchers in Texas and Oklahoma lost 4,000 cattle!

Crimes in Mining Camps

The spot where a miner dug for gold was called his claim. Other people sometimes tried to take over his claim. This was called claim jumping.

 A miner would leave tools in the hole he was digging to show it belonged to him.

Some people even dug tunnels from their claim to someone else's to take their gold! Gunfire broke out in the camps as men fought over claims.

Because there were few rules in a mining camp, mobs of angry and sometimes drunk miners beat up or hanged people they thought were guilty of stealing. But sometimes they were not guilty at all!

The Wild West could be a little *too* exciting. When it got that way, the best thing to do was to head to the sheriff's office for help!

Turn the page to meet some famous lawmen and outlaws.

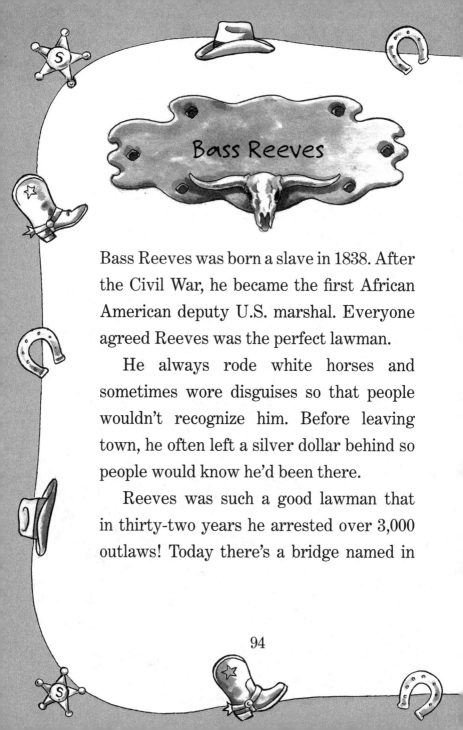

Bass Reeves

Bass Reeves was born a slave in 1838. After the Civil War, he became the first African American deputy U.S. marshal. Everyone agreed Reeves was the perfect lawman.

He always rode white horses and sometimes wore disguises so that people wouldn't recognize him. Before leaving town, he often left a silver dollar behind so people would know he'd been there.

Reeves was such a good lawman that in thirty-two years he arrested over 3,000 outlaws! Today there's a bridge named in his honor in Oklahoma and a statue of him in a park in Fort Smith, Arkansas.

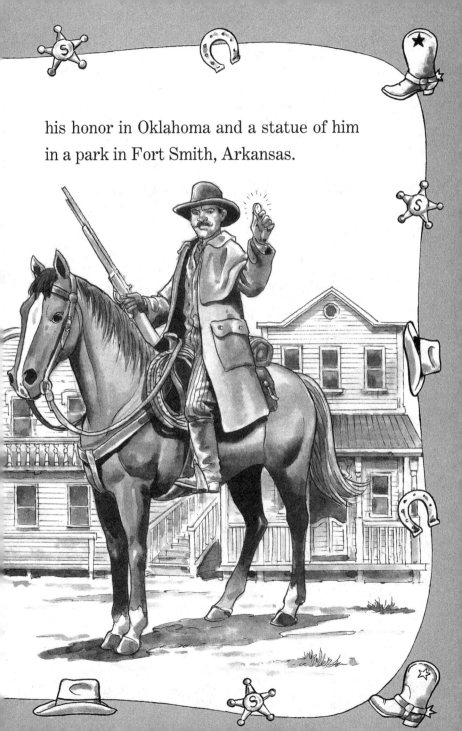

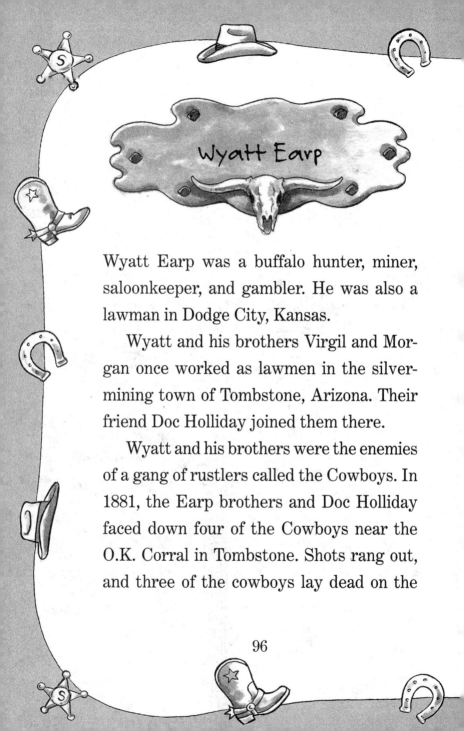

Wyatt Earp

Wyatt Earp was a buffalo hunter, miner, saloonkeeper, and gambler. He was also a lawman in Dodge City, Kansas.

Wyatt and his brothers Virgil and Morgan once worked as lawmen in the silver-mining town of Tombstone, Arizona. Their friend Doc Holliday joined them there.

Wyatt and his brothers were the enemies of a gang of rustlers called the Cowboys. In 1881, the Earp brothers and Doc Holliday faced down four of the Cowboys near the O.K. Corral in Tombstone. Shots rang out, and three of the cowboys lay dead on the

ground. Virgil and Morgan were wounded. The most famous shoot-out in the West—maybe in America—lasted only thirty seconds!

Wyatt later moved to California and worked on movies about the Old West.

Jesse James

Jesse James and his brother, Frank, had a gang called the James-Younger Gang. These outlaws once stopped a train by pulling up a section of tracks! When the train crashed, the men stole money from the safe and gold and jewelry from the passengers.

The James-Younger gang robbed banks, stagecoaches, and trains. They even robbed a county fair! It's thought that Jesse killed twelve people.

The governor of Missouri promised money to anyone who killed Jesse. There were two new members in his gang. One of them shot him to collect the reward. News of Jesse's death spread all over the country. Crowds gathered at his house to see his dead body.

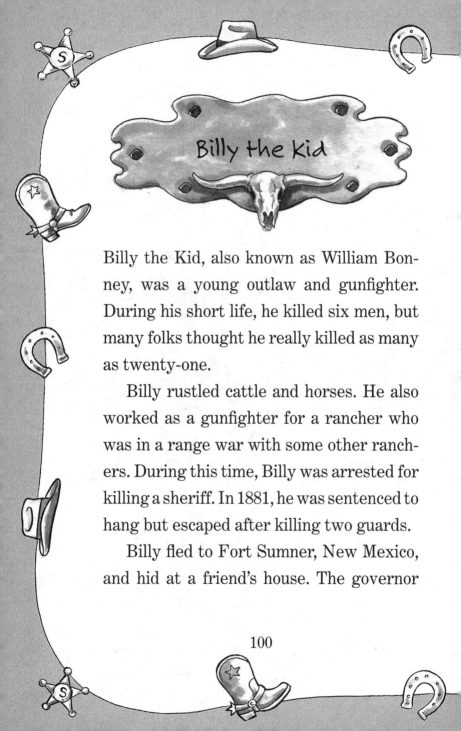

Billy the Kid

Billy the Kid, also known as William Bonney, was a young outlaw and gunfighter. During his short life, he killed six men, but many folks thought he really killed as many as twenty-one.

Billy rustled cattle and horses. He also worked as a gunfighter for a rancher who was in a range war with some other ranchers. During this time, Billy was arrested for killing a sheriff. In 1881, he was sentenced to hang but escaped after killing two guards.

Billy fled to Fort Sumner, New Mexico, and hid at a friend's house. The governor

posted a $500 reward for kiling or cap-
turing him. Sheriff Pat Garrett found out
where Billy was staying and waited for him
there in a darkened room. When Billy came
in, the sheriff fired two times, killing the
outlaw instantly. Billy was only twenty-one
years old.

Wild Bill Hickok

Wild Bill was a stagecoach driver, scout, and gambler. He was also a sheriff and marshal in Kansas. Wild Bill was a gunfighter who once killed a man with only one shot from seventy-five yards away.

He left Kansas and visited a saloon in Deadwood, South Dakota. As he sat at the card table, a man called Jack "Broken Nose" McCall decided to become famous by killing him. He shot Wild Bill in the back of his head, killing him on the spot.

Among the cards Wild Bill was holding were a pair of black aces and a pair of eights. Even today this is known as the Dead Man's Hand.

7

End of the Wild West

By the end of the 1800s, the United States had grown to forty-five states. Settlers had bought up most of the land, and the days of cheap or free land were over. The West was no longer a frontier to be explored and settled.

More trains than ever pulled into little and big towns, sometimes many times a day. And cars were invented!

There were more lawmen and more laws as well. As the cities and towns grew, life became more peaceful.

Wild West Shows

From the late 1880s to the early 1900s, people flocked to Wild West shows. They watched steer roping, sharpshooting, and cowboys doing stunts on horseback. There were even fake stagecoach robberies!

This is an 1899 poster for Buffalo Bill Cody's Wild West show.

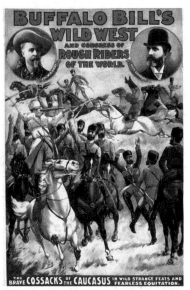

Annie Oakley, who starred in Buffalo Bill's show, could shoot out a candle from ninety feet away!

Buffalo Bill Cody's Wild West show was the most famous. People were excited to watch Native Americans doing dances. To demonstrate the kinds of animals living in the West, Bill brought out buffalo, bears, and a moose. The show even went to England, where the queen watched it three times!

Wild West at the Movies

In the early 1900s, movies had no sound. People read what the actors said on the movie screen. The first western movie was made in 1903. It was a silent film called *The Great Train Robbery*.

In the 1950s and 1960s, kids all over the country went to western movies on Saturday mornings. They followed the adventures of movie cowboys like the Lone Ranger, Roy Rogers, and Gene Autry.

Some of the most famous movie stars

Ronald Reagan was in seven westerns. While he was president, he often went to his ranch in California to relax.

ever were in westerns. John Wayne, who often played a movie cowboy, was one of America's most popular actors. Ronald Reagan, who would become the fortieth president of the United States, was one as well.

There were also tons of TV shows about wagon trains, cowboys, lawmen, and outlaws. For years, Americans were really crazy about the Wild West.

Rodeos

Although there are no more Wild West shows, cowboys and cowgirls can show off their skills at rodeos. They ride bucking horses, rope cows, and wrestle steers to the ground. Many feel that rodeos help keep the spirit of the Wild West alive.

The Real Wild West

Although there were outlaws and lawmen in the Wild West, life there wasn't quite the way movies and TV showed it. There were very few attacks on wagon trains by Native Americans. There weren't even a lot of shoot-outs or robberies. These things all make a good story, but it's not a totally true story.

Most of the time people helped one another. They were brave, worked hard, took care of their families, and obeyed the law. The settlers had big hopes and big dreams, just as we have today. Their spirit and the new lands they dared to settle are an important chapter in the story of America.

Doing More Research

There's a lot more you can learn about the Wild West. The fun of research is seeing how many different sources you can explore.

Books

Most libraries and bookstores have books about the Wild West.

Here are some things to remember when you're using books for research:

1. You don't have to read the whole book. Check the table of contents and the index to find the topics you're interested in.

2. Write down the name of the book.

When you take notes, make sure you write down the name of the book in your notebook so you can find it again.

3. Never copy exactly from a book.

When you learn something new from a book, put it in your own words.

4. Make sure the book is <u>nonfiction</u>.

Some books tell make-believe stories about the Wild West. Make-believe stories are called *fiction*. They're fun to read, but not good for research.

Research books have facts and tell true stories. They are called nonfiction. A librarian or teacher can help you make sure the books you use for research are nonfiction.

Here are some good nonfiction books about the Wild West:

- *Children of the Wild West*
  by Russell Freedman
- *Cowboys of the Wild West*
  by Russell Freedman
- *Daily Life in a Covered Wagon*
  by Paul Erickson
- *Westward Expansion*
  by Teresa Domnauer
- *Who Was Annie Oakley?*
  by Stephanie Spinner
- *Wild West*, a DK Eyewitness book,
  by Stuart Murray
- *You Wouldn't Want to Live in a Wild
  West Town!* by Peter Hicks, illustrated
  by David Antram

Museums

Many museums can help you learn more about the Wild West.

When you go to a museum:

1. Be sure to take your notebook!
Write down anything that catches your interest. Draw pictures, too!

2. Ask questions.
There are almost always people at museums who can help you find what you're looking for.

3. Check the calendar.
Many museums have special events and activities just for kids!

Here are some museums about the
Old West:

- Bisbee Mining and Historical Museum
  (Bisbee, Arizona)
- Cheyenne Frontier Days Old West
  Museum (Cheyenne, Wyoming)
- Kansas Museum of History (Topeka)
- National Cowboy and Western Heritage
  Museum (Oklahoma City)
- National Museum of the American
  Indian (Washington, D.C.)
- National Oregon/California Trail Center
  (Montpelier, Idaho)
- Pioneer Village (Minden, Nebraska)
- Wheelwright Museum of the American
  Indian (Santa Fe, New Mexico)

The Internet

Many websites have lots of facts about the Wild West. Some also have activities that can help make learning about it easier.

Ask your teacher or your parents to help you find more websites like these:

- americanhistory.mrdonn.org /oregontrail.html

- ducksters.com/history /westward_expansion

- montanakids.com/things_to_see_and_do /western_adventure/cattle_drive.htm

- nativeamericans.mrdonn.org /southwest.html

Bibliography

Billington, Ray Allen, and Martin Ridge. *Westward Expansion: A History of the American Frontier.* Albuquerque: University of New Mexico Press, 2009.

Brands, H. W. *The Age of Gold: The California Gold Rush and the New American Dream.* New York: Doubleday, 2002.

Brown, Dee. *The Gentle Tamers: Women of the Old Wild West.* Lincoln: University of Nebraska Press, 1981.

Demlinger, Sandor. *Stagecoach: Rare Views of the Old West, 1849–1915.* Atglen, PA: Schiffer Publishing, 2005.

Hyslop, Stephen G. *The Old West.* Washington, D.C.: National Geographic, 2015.

Marciniak, Kristin. *The Oregon Trail and Westward Expansion.* Ann Arbor, MI: Cherry Lake, 2014.

Philbrick, Nathaniel. *The Last Stand: Custer, Sitting Bull, and the Battle of the Little Bighorn.* New York: Penguin, 2011.

Index

Photographs courtesy of:

Have you read the adventure that matches up with this book?
Don't miss
Magic Tree House® #10
GHOST TOWN AT SUNDOWN

Jack and Annie go back to a spooky ghost town in the Wild West. Will they have time to solve the next tree house riddle? The answer may depend on a ghost!

YOU'LL LOVE FINDING OUT THE FACTS BEHIND THE FICTION IN
Magic Tree House® Fact Tracker

Texas

A NONFICTION COMPANION TO MAGIC TREE HOUSE® #30:
Hurricane Heroes in Texas

When Jack and Annie came back from their
adventure in *Hurricane Heroes in Texas*,
they had a lot of questions.

Why is Texas called the Lone Star State?
What was the Alamo?
When was the Galveston hurricane?
Why was it so terrible?

Find out the answers in Jack and Annie's
very own guide to Texas.

Coming in September 2018!

Magic Tree House®

#1: Dinosaurs Before Dark
#2: The Knight at Dawn
#3: Mummies in the Morning
#4: Pirates Past Noon
#5: Night of the Ninjas
#6: Afternoon on the Amazon
#7: Sunset of the Sabertooth
#8: Midnight on the Moon
#9: Dolphins at Daybreak
#10: Ghost Town at Sundown
#11: Lions at Lunchtime
#12: Polar Bears Past Bedtime
#13: Vacation Under the Volcano
#14: Day of the Dragon King
#15: Viking Ships at Sunrise
#16: Hour of the Olympics
#17: Tonight on the *Titanic*
#18: Buffalo Before Breakfast
#19: Tigers at Twilight
#20: Dingoes at Dinnertime
#21: Civil War on Sunday
#22: Revolutionary War on Wednesday
#23: Twister on Tuesday
#24: Earthquake in the Early Morning
#25: Stage Fright on a Summer Night
#26: Good Morning, Gorillas
#27: Thanksgiving on Thursday
#28: High Tide in Hawaii
#29: A Big Day for Baseball

Magic Tree House® Merlin Missions

#1: Christmas in Camelot
#2: Haunted Castle on Hallows Eve
#3: Summer of the Sea Serpent
#4: Winter of the Ice Wizard
#5: Carnival at Candlelight
#6: Season of the Sandstorms
#7: Night of the New Magicians
#8: Blizzard of the Blue Moon
#9: Dragon of the Red Dawn
#10: Monday with a Mad Genius
#11: Dark Day in the Deep Sea
#12: Eve of the Emperor Penguin
#13: Moonlight on the Magic Flute
#14: A Good Night for Ghosts
#15: Leprechaun in Late Winter
#16: A Ghost Tale for Christmas Time
#17: A Crazy Day with Cobras
#18: Dogs in the Dead of Night
#19: Abe Lincoln at Last!
#20: A Perfect Time for Pandas
#21: Stallion by Starlight
#22: Hurry Up, Houdini!
#23: High Time for Heroes
#24: Soccer on Sunday
#25: Shadow of the Shark
#26: Balto of the Blue Dawn
#27: Night of the Ninth Dragon

Magic Tree House®
Super Editions

#1: World at War, 1944

Magic Tree House®
Fact Trackers

Dinosaurs

Knights and Castles

Mummies and Pyramids

Pirates

Rain Forests

Space

Titanic

Twisters and Other Terrible Storms

Dolphins and Sharks

Ancient Greece and the Olympics

American Revolution

Sabertooths and the Ice Age

Pilgrims

Ancient Rome and Pompeii

Tsunamis and Other Natural Disasters

Polar Bears and the Arctic

Sea Monsters

Penguins and Antarctica

Leonardo da Vinci

Ghosts

Leprechauns and Irish Folklore

Rags and Riches: Kids in the Time of Charles Dickens

Snakes and Other Reptiles

Dog Heroes

Abraham Lincoln

Pandas and Other Endangered Species

Horse Heroes

Heroes for All Times

Soccer

Ninjas and Samurai

China: Land of the Emperor's Great Wall

Sharks and Other Predators

Vikings

Dogsledding and Extreme Sports

Dragons and Mythical Creatures

World War II

Baseball

Wild West

More Magic Tree House®

Games and Puzzles from the Tree House

Magic Tricks from the Tree House

My Magic Tree House Journal

Magic Tree House Survival Guide

Animals Games and Puzzles

Magic Tree House Incredible Fact Book

**Continue
the adventure with
Jack and Annie!**

Use your exclusive code
below to unlock
special content at
**MagicTreeHouse.com/
exclusives.**

MERLIN